ROAD TRANSPORT MONMOUTHSHIRE
by
Paul Heaton

P.M. Heaton Publishing
Abergavenny Monmouthshire
Great Britain
2005

Front Cover: This ERF 32 tonnes GVW 8wl tipper was supplied to W.J. Clayton & Sons Ltd., Rogerstone, by Richard Read (Commercials) Ltd., Longhope, hence the Gloucestershire registration number: P855UDD.

Title Page: This Thornycroft 8wl flat, HAX970 was one of three of this type which passed to British Road Services with the rest of the Tim Price fleet when nationalised in 1949.

Back Cover: A 1980s view of the fleet of Cliff Stephens Transport Ltd., Griffithstown, Pontypool.

ISBN 1 872006 19 1

© First Edition October, 2005

Published by P.M. Heaton Publishing
Abergavenny, Monmouthshire, NP7 8NG

Printed in Great Britain by
The Amadeus Press Ltd.,
Cleckheaton, West Yorkshire, BD19 4TQ

Typesetting and page layout by
Highlight Type Bureau Ltd., Bradford BD8 7BY

CONTENTS

Seen at the lorry wash at Abergavenny Cattle Market this Scania 124L 6x2 tractor unit W257NTG was bought new by Llantilio Transport. Coupled to an aluminium four deck stock trailer it is driven by John Pritchard of Abergavenny.

PREFACE

In this further volume in my 'Road Transport' series I have included transport contractors operating in the old County of Monmouthshire involved with general haulage, steel traffic, quarry and site tippers and livestock haulage. Happily a number of these businesses survive today, but alas details of the last steel coil to be transported from Panteg Steelworks on March 19, 2004, are given.

I am grateful to all those who have kindly helped with photographs and information, including Richard Clayton, Gordon Clayton, Mrs. Felicity Davies, Robert Davies, John Fletcher, Bill Gibbon, John Gibbon, Derek Griffiths, Richard Griffiths, R. W. Jenkins, David Llewellyn, Gwyn Llewellyn, Frank Lonney, Dario Passaro, Christopher Stedman, Philip Stedman, Robert Stedman, Clarry Whistance and Mrs. Edna Whistance. To anyone else who has helped – thank you.

To the reader, I hope you enjoy the book – another look back in time.

Paul Heaton
Abergavenny
October, 2005

Little Oaks, Rhiwderin – base for the W. J. Clayton & Sons fleet for 85 years to 2000. Three ERF 'E' Series 8wl tippers are seen with Leyland Constructor 8wl and 6wl tippers.

W. J. CLAYTON & SONS (KELVEDON TRANSPORT CO. LTD.), ROGERSTONE

William James Clayton came to Monmouthshire from Hadley in Shropshire to take up employment at the Rogerstone Steelworks of Nettlefolds, better known later as Guest, Keen & Nettlefolds. In 1911 he bought a horse and cart and started hauling bricks from Risca, and much of the material used in building Park Avenue and Church Street, Rogerstone was carried by him.

In 1916 he moved to a yard at 'Little Oaks', Rhiwderin which was rented from Tredegar Estate, and was to be the home of the business for the next 85 years, and was bought in 1952. He expanded with horse-drawn vehicles and his work included bricks from Risca, pipes for the Gas Works, and in the summer months was also employed drawing a water bowser for wetting the dusty roads which had yet to be tarmaced.

He was soon joined by his son, also called William James Clayton, who was a professional footballer and prize fighter – he would fight anyone for money, and often did.

Expansion continued, and a coal round was undertaken in the locality, and whilst the horse and cart was to continue to be used until 1951, in 1923 they obtained their first petrol-engined lorry, a Chevrolet with solid tyres from Atlas Garages at Newport for £215. This vehicle and subsequent acquisitions were employed mainly on tipper work, bricks, chippings and stone out of Cwm Leycyon Quarry, Draethen. Thereafter they operated tippers out of the quarries owned by Powell Duffryn, Wm. Adams, United Transport Quarries and Hodson Concrete.

A third generation of the family entered the business, when William's sons – Bill (William), Dick (Richard) and Gordon arrived.

GKN had left Castle Works at Rogerstone and in 1938 Hinkin & Frewin had the contract to build a new factory on the site for the Air Ministry. The firm were to haul all the steelwork to the site used in the construction and when sold in 1946 to Northern Aluminium they became important customers. Castle Works, now owned by Alcan Rolled Products, continue to provide regular employment for the business and Claytons' pride themselves on the standard of service and loyalty they give.

In 1962 the business was incorporated as W.J. Clayton & Sons Ltd., and shortly after they acquired the Newport haulage business of Kelvedon Transport Co. Ltd. Kelvedon's were operating tippers nationwide transporting animal waste and bones for British Glue. This called for considerable investment, and eventually 22 long wheelbased 4wl tippers fitted with aluminium bodies were employed, and facilities were taken up for this large fleet at Market Harborough, Dudley, Liverpool and London. Eventually the customer became Croda, and they were responsible for all manner of products from fertilizers to cosmetics.

The benefit of this work was the vehicles were always loaded, but when changes were effected which meant the vehicles were running long distances empty, this severely effected the profitability of the work, and in consequence they withdrew from this business.

Quarry tipper work continued, and in the late 1960s they took over the running of the Monmouthshire Tipper Group from Wynns. This called for the organising of work for 400 vehicles, and they continued with this until it was wound up. They ran the Brynmawr based tipper fleet of Ford & Reames, and took over the businesses and fleets of Harold Sergeant and Bernard Russell, both of Risca. They also founded with others the Heads of the Valleys Training School at Gilwern.

They moved into articulation, and found work with Whitehead Iron & Steel, Goddins, Broads Manhole Covers, Richard Thomas & Baldwin (later British Steel Corporation) at Llanwern, and the Ministry of Defence at Glascoed, among others.

With the advent of central heating, the use of domestic coal was considerably reduced, and in 1991 this part of the business was sold.

Bill's son Tony (William Anthony) spent 26 years in the business and thereafter ran a household removal business together with a single tipper for his own account. Dick's son Gerald spent eighteen years in the business, whilst his brothers Richard and Robin together with Gordon's son Paul now run the firm.

Having sold the 'Little Oaks' site for building development, on January 1, 2000 they marked the New Millennium by moving to new purpose built premises at Wern Industrial Estate, Rogerstone, which is appropriately named 'Little Oaks Garage'.

Flexibility has been a feature of the firm's history, which has meant of late, a contraction of the tipper work, with an expansion of the general haulage business. Currently a modern fleet of around thirty vehicles is operated, with substantially more sem-trailers.

FLEET LIST

Index No.	Make & Type	Work
NDW380	Commer 6wl flat	General
RWO827	Commer 4wl flat	General
RAX908	AEC 4wl flat	Northern Aluminium colours
RDG473	Bedford 'S' type	General
PWO97	Bedford 'S' type	General
RAX409	Bedford 'S' type	General
SCJ447	Commer 4wl tipper	Quarry/site
TAX284	Bedford 4wl flat	Contract
VWO321	Bedford 4wl tipper	Quarry/site
UDW59	Commer 4wl tipper	Raw bone
XAX478	Bedford 4wl tipper	Quarry/site
XAX794	Bedford 4wl dropside flat	Contract
YWO550	Bedford 4wl tipper	Contract
YWO627	Bedford 4wl tipper	Contract
731VPG	Massey Ferguson tractor	Loader
WDW482	Commer 6wl flat	General
732AWO	Bedford 4wl flat	General
578AWO	Bedford 4wl flat	General
966AWO	Bedford 4wl tipper	Contract
779BAX	Albion 4x2 tractor unit	General
563BWO	Bedford 4wl tipper	Quarry/site
604BWO	Leyland 4x2 tractor unit	General
71CAX	Leyland 4x2 tractor unit	General
745CAX	Albion 6wl flat	General
YDW663	Leyland Comet 4x2 tractor unit	Alcan colours
YDW921	Commer 4wl flat	General
YDW923	Leyland 4x2 tractor unit	Alcan colours
1063DW	Commer 6wl tipper	Raw bone
454CWO	Leyland Comet 4x2 tractor unit	Alcan colours
883CWO	Bedford 4wl tipper	Quarry/site
102DAX	Leyland Comet 4x2 tractor unit	Alcan colours
103DAX	Leyland Comet 4x2 tractor unit	Alcan colours
716DAX	Bedford 4wl tipper	Quarry/site
242FAX	Bedford 4wl tipper	Site

Index No.	Make & Type	Work
957FAX	Bedford 4x2 tractor unit	General
72PAE		
DFB76	AEC 4x2 tractor unit	General
956FAX	Bedford 4x2 tractor unit	General
958FAX	Bedford 4x2 tractor unit	General
2374DW	Commer 4wl flat	Dry bone - bagged
3238DW	Commer 4wl flat	General
BOR64		
4227DW	Commer 6wl flat	General
AAX644B	Bedford 4wl tipper	Raw bone
AWO194B	Bedford 4wl tipper	Raw bone
AWO272B	Bedford 4wl tipper	Raw bone
BWO694B	Bedford 4wl flat	General
CAX261B	Bedford 4wl tipper	Raw bone
BDE333C	Leyland 4x2 tractor unit	General
FFM246C		
DAX919C	Bedford 4wl tipper	Quarry/site
EQO225C	Bedford 4wl tipper	Quarry/site
FWO392C	Bedford 4wl flat	General
HWO922D	Bedford 4wl tipper	Quarry/site
JAX856D	Leyland 4x2 tractor unit	General
JWO914D	Leyland Comer 4x2 tractor unit	General
LAX455E	Bedford KM 4wl tipper	Raw bone
ONY449E	Bedford KM 4wl tipper	Quarry/site
KKG23E	Austin van	Service vehicle
KRR103E	Leyland 4wl tipper	Quarry/site
GBX387E	AEC 4x2 tractor unit	General
NTN637E	Leyland Beaver 4x2 tractor unit	General
MTN967E	Leyland 4x2 tractor unit	General
JUH330E	Leyland 4x2 tractor unit	General
NAX832F	Bedford KM 4wl tipper	Raw bone
PAX128F	Bedford KM 4wl tipper	Raw bone
PAX928F	Leyland 4x2 tractor unit	General
ONY734F	Leyland 4wl flat	General
LDE555F	Leyland 4x2 tractor unit	General
MCY366F	Leyland 4wl tipper	Quarry/site
VUW566G	Ford D1000 4wl tipper	Raw bone

Index No.	Make & Type	Work
VUW580G	Ford D1000 4wl tipper	Raw bone
VUW581G	Ford D1000 4wl tipper	Raw bone
VUW582G	Ford D1000 4wl tipper	Raw bone
LBX256G	Albion	
RAX423G	Albion 4wl flat	General
RWO308G	Seddon 4wl flat	General
SAX23G	Albion 4wl tipper	Quarry/site
SAX24G	Albion 4wl flat	General
SAX881G	Albion 4wl tipper	Raw bone
SWO527G	Albion 4wl tipper	Raw bone
SWO883G	Leyland 4wl tipper	Quarry/site
TAX250G	Seddon 4wl flat	General
SOW843H	Leyland 4x2 tractor unit	General
TCY310H	Leyland Beaver 4x2 tractor unit	General
TWO188H	Albion 4wl tipper	Quarry/site
TWO583H	Albion 4wl tipper	Raw bone
UAX232H	Albion 4wl tipper	Raw bone
UAX623H	Albion 4wl tipper	Raw bone
UAX924H	Seddon 4wl tipper	Quarry/site
VWO297J	Albion 4wl tipper	Raw bone
VWO538H	Leyland 4wl tipper	Quarry/site
XAX428J	Leyland 4wl tipper	Raw bone
XAX429J	Leyland 4x2 tractor unit	General
XWO131J	Leyland 4x2 tractor unit	General
KVD699L	Leyland Reiver 6x2 tipper	Quarry/site
PYL188L	Leyland Reiver 6x2 tipper	Quarry/site
PWO216M	Scammell 4x2 tractor unit	General
RTX449M	Leyland Reiver 6x2 tipper	Quarry/site
ARD475M	Leyland Reiver 6x2 tipper	Quarry/site
GWO211N	Leyland Badger 4x2 tractor unit	General
NCY628R	Leyland Reiver 6x2 tipper	Quarry/site
OOU149R	ERF B Series 4x2 tractor unit	General
STX952S	Leyland Reiver 6x2 tipper	Quarry/site
TUH661S	Leyland Reiver 6x2 tipper	Quarry/site
TBO301S	Leyland Reiver 6x2 tipper	Quarry/site
VDA341S	Leyland Reiver 6x2 tipper	Quarry/site
XNY467T	Leyland Reiver 6x2 tipper	Quarry/site

Index No.	Make & Type	Work
YBO669T	ERF B Series 6x2 tractor unit	General
AAX818T	ERF B Series 6x2 tractor unit	General
DUH66V	ERF B Series 4x2 tractor unit	General
DUH67V	ERF B Series 4x2 tractor unit	General
XCX396V	ERF B Series 8x4 tipper	Quarry/site
PHW374W	Leyland 4wl flat	Coal delivery
JWO252W	Leyland Marathon 4x2 tractor unit	General
JWO253W	Leyland Marathon 4x2 tractor unit	General
LHB311X	Leyland Marathon 4x2 tractor unit	Bulk tipper
MUH138X	Leyland Constructor 8x4 tipper	Quarry/site
UFX821X	Leyland Constructor 8x4 tipper	Quarry/site
RUH439Y	Leyland Constructor 8x4 tipper	Quarry/site
RUH440Y	Leyland Marathon 4x2 tractor unit	General
EYD198Y	Leyland Constructor 6x2 tipper	Quarry/site
A193UUH	Leyland Constructor 6x2 tipper	Quarry/site
A329SAE	Leyland Constructor 8x4 tipper	Quarry/site
A45HNE	ERF C Series 4x2 tractor unit	General
A742WBO	ERF C Series 4x2 tractor unit	General
B330BF	Leyland Constructor 6x2 tipper	Quarry/site
B34TBO	Leyland Constructor 6x2 tipper	Quarry/site
B491ANY	ERF C Series 4x2 tractor unit	General
B198CHB	ERF C Series 4x2 tractor unit	General
C921XDD	ERF E Series 4x2 tractor unit	General
C922XDD	ERF E Series 4x2 tractor unit	General
D903NHB	ERF E Series 4x2 tractor unit	General
D353XJU	ERF E Series 4x2 tractor unit	General
D489SFM	ERF E Series 4x2 tractor unit	General
E214LEU	Leyland Constructor 6x4 tipper	Quarry/site
E49SNY	ERF E Series 8x4 tipper	Quarry/site
E50SNY	ERF E Series 4x2 tractor unit	General
F617KAO	ERF E Series 4x2 tractor unit	General
F725XTG	ERF E Series 4x2 tractor unit	General
F285AHB	ERF E Series 4x2 tractor unit	General
F286AHB	ERF E Series 4x2 tractor unit	General
F512BUH	ERF E Series 6x4 tipper	Quarry/site
F877VCV	Leyland Constructor 6x4 tipper	Quarry/site
G816RNE	ERF E Series 8x4 tipper	Quarry/site

Index No.	Make & Type	Work
G510GHB	ERF E Series 4x2 tractor unit	General
H219PKG	ERF E Series 4x2 tractor unit	General
H995YMB	ERF E Series 8x4 tipper	Quarry/site
J960GLG	ERF E Series 8x4 tipper	Quarry/site
K698XWO	Leyland Constructor 8x4 tipper	Quarry/site
K709XWO	ERF E Series 4x2 tractor unit	General
L142EHB	ERF E Series 8x4 tipper	Quarry/site
M113LNE	ERF E Series 8x4 tipper	Quarry/site
M446PKN	ERF EC 6x2 tractor unit	General
N225SVP	ERF EC 6x2 tractor unit	General
N370OBO	ERF EC 4x2 tractor unit	General
N694ODG	ERF EC 4x2 tractor unit	General
N157GJO	Leyland Daf 6wl tipper	Quarry/site
P59PVT	ERF EC 4x2 tractor unit	General
P855UDD	ERF 8x4 tipper	Quarry/site
P986PRF	ERF EC 6x2 tractor unit	General
P844WTX	Leyland Daf 4x2 tractor unit	General
R918BTG	ERF EC 4x2 tractor unit	General
R919BTG	ERF EC 4x2 tractor unit	General
S928JDD	ERF EC 4x2 tractor unit	General
S173COJ	ERF EC 6x2 tractor unit	General
S687VKL	ERF 8x4 tipper	Quarry/site
T470AJF	ERF EC 4x2 tractor unit	General
V223EAD	ERF EC 6x2 tractor unit	General
V850HTG	Daf 6x2 tractor unit	General
W269NTG	Daf 6x2 tractor unit	General
W544DKE	ERF EC 6x2 tractor unit	General
W187PKS	MAN 6x4 tipper	Quarry/site
X445CMB	ERF EC 6x2 tractor unit	General
Y982RDF	ERF EC 6x2 tractor unit	General
Y369HAE	ERF EC 8x4 tipper	Quarry/site
SF51LZB	Daf 6x2 tractor unit	General
CK02VHE	Foden 6x2 tractor unit	General
CN04EWM	ERF 6x2 tractor unit	General

Above: William James Clayton (son of the founder) and Tommy Andrews seen with the first motor lorry, a Chevrolet, bought new in 1923 from Atlas Garages, Newport.

Below: Eldest grandson Bill is seen on the coal round with an early Bedford dropside. Fred Archer is in the background.

Three Bedford 'S' type dropside lorries in the mid-1950s – RDG473, PW097 and RAX409.

This AEC Mercury 4wl flat, RAX908 bought new in 1957 was on contract to Northern Aluminium at Rogerstone.

An early view of the workshops at Little Oaks, Rhiwderin.

The laden Leyland 4wl flat ONY734F can be identified in this group of vehicles in the workshops.

Frank Lonney was the driver of one of these Bedford TK
tippers working on-site when he took these photographs.
Opposite top: Bernard Harding is seen with these two
Bedfords, dating from 1961 – 883CWO and 563BWO.

Opposite bottom: Walter Legg infront of this 1964 Bedford
AWO272B.

Above: John Burns in the cab of Bedford TK, 883CWO
which whilst tipping has gone over backwards into a deep
trench.

Risca Carnival. Two of the general haulage fleet articulated outfits join in.
Above: Albion 779BAX of 1961. *Below*: Leyland Super Comet JWO914D.

This Scammell articulated tractor unit PWO216M was part of an expanding general haulage fleet.

The waiting area at Machen Quarry. In the background is Clayton's Leyland Reiver 6wl tipper TBO301S driven by Richard Clayton (Dick's son) awaiting his turn to load.

W. J. Clayton & Sons Ltd., operated a large fleet of tippers on site work and hauling from quarries. Gradually the size of individual vehicles was increased from 4 wheelers to 8 wheelers.

Whilst they operated ten 6x2 Leyland Reivers', the fleet was uprated initially with five Leyland Constructor 8x4 tippers and two 6x4 and two 6x2 from the same manufacturer.

The first 8 wheeler to be owned by Claytons' was this Constructor MUH138X which arrived in 1981. It is seen here loading on August 5, 1982 at the Hafod Quarry, Abercarn whilst driven by Richard Clayton.

Subsequently they were to operate a fleet of ten 8wl ERF double-drive tippers on this work, together with single ERF, Leyland Daf and MAN six wheelers.

Leyland 8wl tipper MUH138X is seen at Cwmbran Drive in March, 1983.

This Leyland 6wl tipper is seen at Cwmbran Drive in June, 1983.

W. J. Clayton & Sons core activities were general haulage with articulated outfits and quarry and site work with appropriate tippers. Whilst they occassionally brought a load of coal back to Rhiwderin for their ever reducing household coal business, they did not actually own a bulk tipper suitable for the normal transport of coal. It came as something of a surprise during the 1984/85 Miner's Strike when the Transport & General Workers Union accused the firm of carrying coal and coke in the convoys running from Port Talbot to British Steel at Llanwern. This statement, which was untrue, wa subsequently withdrawn. However an arson attack took place at their Rhiwderin yard involving three of their Leyland Reivers' two of which were so badly damaged that they were written-off. The other was subsequently repaired. As a result Claytons' immediately bought a Leyland Marathon tractor unit and bulk tipper trailer and within 48 hours the vehicle was placed in the convoys from Port Talbot to Llanwern. They had no need or want to be involved in this traffic – but once their vehicles had been attacked for absolutely no reason – they put the one vehicle on this job in retaliation.

The coal and coke convoy running from Port Talbot to Llanwern Steelworks during the 1984/85 Miner's Strike. Following an arson attack on three of their vehicles they bought this Leyland Marathon bulk tipper outfit LHB331X and ran it on this job. The vehicle is seen at the end of this line of vehicles near Pound Hill, Castleton on the M4 Motorway.

This Leyland Constructor 6wl tipper B33OBF is seen:
Above: at Cwmbran Drive in November, 1993, and
Below: at Newbridge in March, 1994.

Leyland 6wl tipper E214LEU at Cwmbran Drive in June, 1993.

Leyland tipper A193UUH at Newbridge in March, 1994.

Leyland Constructor 6wl tipper F877VCV, seen –
Above: at Cwmbran Drive in May, 1994. Below: at the M4 Magor Service Area – May, 1997.
Opposite top: on Cardiff Road, Newport, near Belle Vue Park, in May, 1998.
Opposite bottom: at the new Little Oaks Garage, Rogerstone post-2000.

In the early 1960s Claytons' bought the Newport haulage business of Kelvedon Transport Co. Ltd. and initially operated tippers on raw bone transport. When this work was given up thereafter the general haulage fleet was operated under Kelvedons' name, whereas the tipper business was carried on under the original firm. This ERF 'C' Series B198CHB is involved with a local carnival.

This pair of ERFs was supplied by Richard Read (Commercials) Ltd., Longhope.

Winter and Summer at Little Oaks Garage, Rhiwderin. The expanding ERF general haulage fleet.

ERF E10, D903NHB finished in the colours of Kelvedon Transport.

D353YJU shown at the new Little Oaks Garage at Rogerstone.

The Kelvedon general haulage fleet was virtually standardised on the ERF model. This E14, F617KAO dated from 1989.

ERF – F286AHB was supplied by South Wales Commercials, Newport.

Opposite top: ERF F725XTG is seen with D903NHB.

Opposite bottom: ERF G510GHB

Above: ERF tractor unit, F285AHB. Kelvedon Transport operated ERFs with a variety of engines and whilst Cummins predominated, the Rolls Royce Eagle engine was also highly thought of.

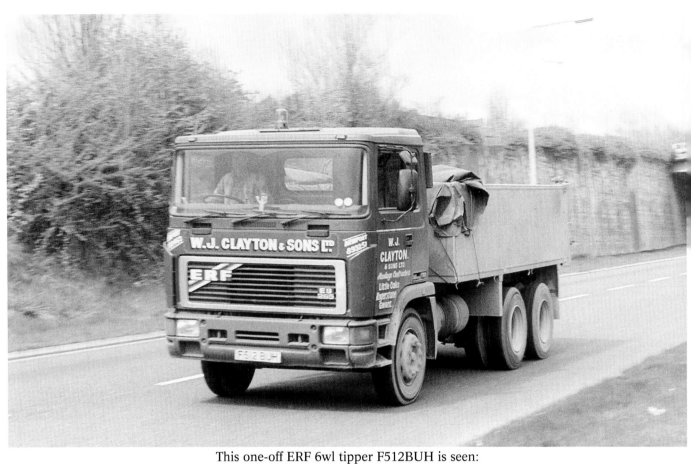

This one-off ERF 6wl tipper F512BUH is seen:
Above: at Cwmbran Drive in April, 1994, and
Below: at the M4 Motorway Services at Magor in February, 1997.

This ERF 'E' Series 8wl tipper, E49SNY is seen at New Inn, near Pontypool in June, 1994.

Kelvedon Transport's ERF – E14 with tri-axle trailer. (G510GHB).

ERF 8wl tipper G816RNE shown (*above*) at the M4 Motorway Cardiff West Services in March, 1997, and (*below*) at Newport in July, 1997.

W. J. Clayton & Sons' ERF 8wl tipper H995YMB seen (*above*) at the Little Oaks premises at Rogerstone and (*below*) at Cwmbran Drive, in the Eastern Valley of Monmouthshire in May, 1993.

ERF – J960GLG seen (*above*) at Little Oaks, Rhiwderin, and (*below*) at Cwmbran in April, 1994. All the tippers in the Clayton fleet were fitted with insulated bodywork for the carriage of hot tarmac for use in road surfacing.

This ERF 8wl tipper K698XWO is seen (above) at Llantarnam in April, 1995 and (below) at Cwmbran in March, 1996.

Seen at the Little Oaks Garage at Rogerstone this ERF 8wl double drive tipper was fitted with the 325 bhp Rolls Royce engine.

Another ERF 8wl tipper, L142EHB seen at Newport in July, 1997.

Seen in November, 1995 – ERF M113LNE. During the Foot & Mouth Outbreak a number of
these tippers were employed transporting animal carcesses for disposal for the Ministry of Agriculture, Fisheries
and Food (MAFF), later DEFRA.

Dick Clayton on the left and Gordon Clayton second from right seen with the workshop staff.

Leyland Daf 6wl tipper N157GJO.

ERF EC11 6x2 tractor unit P986PRF at Rogerstone.

Rare Leyland Daf tractor unit P844WTX.

ERF EC14 6x2 tractor unit M446PKN with curtainsider trailer.

ERF EC11 tractor unit R918BTG at Rogerstone.

ERF EC11 tractor unit R918BTG with triaxle trailer laden with aluminium ingot for Alcan at Rogerstone.

This ERF EC11 R919BTG is seen on the outskirts of Rogerstone.

This ERF 8wl tipper operating at 32 tonnes GVW is fitted with the Perkins engine.

Kelvedon Transport's ERF EC11 tractor unit S928JDD.

This Foden 6x2 tractor unit CK02VHE is seen on the weighbridge at the Alcan Factory in Bridgnorth in 2004.

LEN DAVIES, CROSS ASH

Leonard Frederick Alick Davies was born at Abergavenny on October 7th, 1928. Living at Ross Road, Abergavenny, he spent all his time on Market Days in and around the Cattle Market, and at the end of the sale helped drove the animals to the pens at the railway station and assisted in loading them onto goods wagons for onward transport by rail. That was the way it was done in those days.

Leaving school he worked locally for a while, but as soon as he was old enough passed his driving test on a stock lorry of E.R. Clissold of Mount Street, Abergavenny, for whom he was to work for a while. Thereafter he drove for SHACS (South Herefordshire Agricultural Cooperative Society) of Cross Street, Abergavenny, delivering animal feedstuffs and the like to the farming community in the area. From there he went driving another stock lorry – with Charlie Bailey (who had formerly traded as Marshall & Bailey) of Pandy.

Whilst farming wasn't his background, he was becoming well-known throughout the industry in the area. This was to be important.

In 1965 he married Felicity Jones of The Gables, Cross Ash, and they made their home there, and had two children Deborah and Robert Leonard.

In 1971 he entered business on his own account with a small Bedford stock lorry which he bought off Charlie Bailey. After a short time he entered into partnership with Clive Powell who owned Brynmawr Slaughter House. Trading as L & C Transport they bought two brand new stock lorries, both four wheelers, an Albion and a Leyland. The Leyland, whilst having wooden decks, was one of the first in the area with an aluminium body. Within two years he was on his own, and using the Leyland which was his part of the dissolved partnership.

He bought another vehicle which John Malnati drove, and eventually daughter Deborah drove a small stock lorry, remaining with her father for about seven years. Son Rob worked in a garage when he left school, and on passing his driving test in 1991 went to work for his father. Shortly after, they bought a Daf 6wl stock lorry and drawbar trailer, which enabled them to carry the full possible load, giving the maximum 48ft of platform space.

Sadly in April, 1994 Len Davies died unexpectedly – but will always be remembered for his cheerful, straight-talking personality. Thereafter his widow Flick (Felicity) and son Rob carried on the business, expanding and changing direction when required. They acquired articulated outfits when this was needed, and survived the difficult period of the 'Foot & Mouth Outbreak' managing to find some flat work and used a 6wl Volvo with the box removed on similar traffic.

They are now operating maximum capacity articulated outfits together with a Volvo drawbar outfit and a useful 4wl Volvo for smaller loads. Paul Holland, John Malnati, Colin Richards and Rob carry out the driving together with a small number of well qualified locals with Flick still very much actively involved in the business.

For a year or so from 1972 Len Davies was in partnership with Clive Powell of Brynmawr Slaughter House operating this pair of stock lorries, an Albion with aluminium box and Leyland with wooden body.

Opposite top: This Daf RHW212S is seen at The Gables, Cross Ash.

Opposite bottom: A useful vehicle for smaller loads was this Bedford TK, WMG 398T.

This DAF 2500 6wl livestock transporter B80AOC and drawbar trailer is seen (*above*) at Hereford Market and (*below*) undertaking a long climb on the open road.

Len Davies with his son Rob.

Seen at The Gablers, Cross Ash this Bedford TK, WVC352X was fitted with an aluminium stock box.

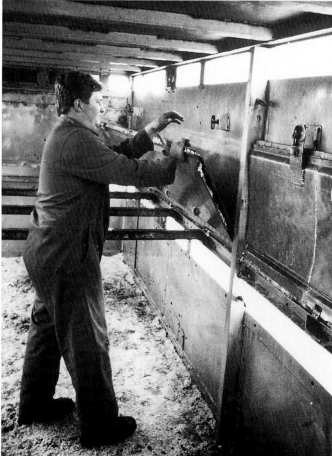

Opposite top left: Cattle being unloaded from the Daf, B80AOC.

Opposite top right: Rob Davies loading ewes.

Opposite bottom and above: Rob Davies sets up the three-deck body of the Daf B80AOC using liberal amounts of sawdust.

This pair of Volvo FL10 6wl livestock lorries E966WWL and G185SJO were often used with drawbar trailers.

This Volvo FL6 H381AGB was originally an articulated tractor unit which was stretched and fitted with a livestock box. It is seen above at the Gables, Cross Ash and below at Abergavenny Cattle Market.

Seen at Abergavenny Cattle Market this 6wl Volvo FH12, S366JNW is often used as a drawbar outfit and is driven by John Malnati.

This Scania 124L, R867CVV is seen on the Lorry Wash at Abergavenny Cattle Market.

Daf 95XF, R4ACT is pictured at The Gables, Cross Ash.

D.R. GRIFFITHS (E. & O. GRIFFITHS), DINGESTOW, MONMOUTH

Enoch William Griffiths operated from Efailnewydd (translated 'New Blacksmith Shop'), Dingestow, near Monmouth from the last quarter of the 19th Century. His activities were wide, and included Agricultural Engineering, operating threshing machines, haulage and as a blacksmith, and owned a Wallis-Stevens traction engine 'Sally'.

William, as he was better known, had four children, two sons and two daughters. The eldest son Enoch learnt his trade as an engineer with Wilks of Little Mill and the younger Oliver trained as a blacksmith. With the early death of their father, they set up business as blacksmiths at Dingestow, and thereinafter traded as E. & O. Griffiths. They quickly expanded and took another Blacksmith's Shop at Dingestow, soon employing four men qualified in the trade.

However, having an eye to the future, they saw the developments in road haulage, and decided to invest. Their first lorry was a Willys-Overland Crossley which was to carry out hiring-work for Monmouth District Council from the early 1930s. The success of this venture saw the purchase of a secondhand Sentinel DG6 6 wheel tipper, DG3171 followed by a Foden 'Speed 6' 4 wheel tipper, WO5273. These early vehicles found employment carrying bricks from Sirhowy to Brecon, Builth Wells, Leominster, and the surrounding areas. Possibly their main customer was to be Monmouthshire Council who owned Cwmynyscoy Quarry near Pontypool, and from early in 1934 considerable amounts of material were carried on their behalf mainly to the Monmouth, Abergavenny and Skenfrith areas for road construction and repair.

They next bought a Marshall (Marshalls of Gainsborough) steam traction engine, WO6679, which arrived at Monmouth by rail and was immediately used on threshing for a Mr. Watkins at Deepholm Farm. This machine was to see continuous employment right up to and throughout the Second World War.

In 1934 E. & O. Griffiths purchased an 8 wheel Sentinel S8 steam lorry, UJ3652. This vehicle was a flatbed, and was an ex-demonstrator model acquired through Wm. Fish of Bristol. Due to objections to the licensing authority from Robert Wynn & Sons Ltd., Newport, this vehicle was placed on contract to Freeguard Brothers Transport of Newport, and was used on hauling steel out of South Wales.

The brothers were very progressive in their outlook, and quickly saw the future in haulage with the petrol engine; thus they acquired a Crossley 4 wheel tipper, which saw service carrying bricks from Ebbw Vale and the Valleys to all parts of South Wales and the South West.

This was followed by a Leyland Beaver, a Leyland Bull, two Leyland Cubs, two Leyland Lynx, an early Leyland Comet and a host of Bedfords. They were all tippers, and by the war sixteen lorries were being used.

Alas nothing lasts for ever, and in the late 1940s the business was nationalised by the government.

Having hauled out of Cwmynyscoy Quarry for almost twenty years, when Monmouthshire County Council decided to sell it, the brothers bought and operated it for a further two decades until they finally decided to retire, when it was disposed of.

Around 1950 Oliver's son Derek had completed his National Service with the RAF, and on return home took up employment with British Road Services as a driver, whilst his brother John took up farming.

The Griffiths brothers had always insured their vehicles with the Sea Insurance Company of Cardiff, and it was their manager Ronald Taylor who told Oliver about a haulage business which was for sale due to bankruptcy. There was a fleet of seven vehicles which had been operating carrying shale for Star Brick & Tile – consisting of three QX Commers, a Q4 Commer, two Dodge Kews and a Canadian Ford, all tippers. This entire fleet was acquired by Derek, with support from his father, for £3,500.

Thus D.R. Griffiths entered business on his own account, operating as earlier generations, from Dingestow. Whilst useful employment was secured from Cwmynyscoy Quarry, other work consisted of sand from Newport, bricks for Little Mill Brick Co. Ltd., and included work from various quarries, including Cleerwell Quarry and Whitecliffe Quarry, Gloucestershire.

Important revenue was obtained with vehicles on day work to Monmouthshire County Council Highways Department, and the fleet was to comprise Bedford, Dodge, Leyland, AEC, Atkinson and Seddon Atkinson.

The operating base was moved to Drybridge Garage, Wonastow Road, Monmouth, where Derek's son Richard was subsequently to take over, and gradually the haulage business was reduced. However, the long serving driver Malcolm Price was to drive their sole surviving vehicle, usually on Llanwern Slag, this being an 8wl Seddon Atkinson tipper.

When Derek retired, Malcolm then worked for his sons, at first from 1988 with a Foden 6wl tipper, but latterly with an ERF 6wl tipper still hauling for Llanwern Slag. Alas around 1995 Malcolm Price died, tragically before retirement, and the final lorry was disposed of.

Today, the Drybridge Garage is run by Derek's son Richard, whilst his twin brother Andrew has followed a career in the civil service.

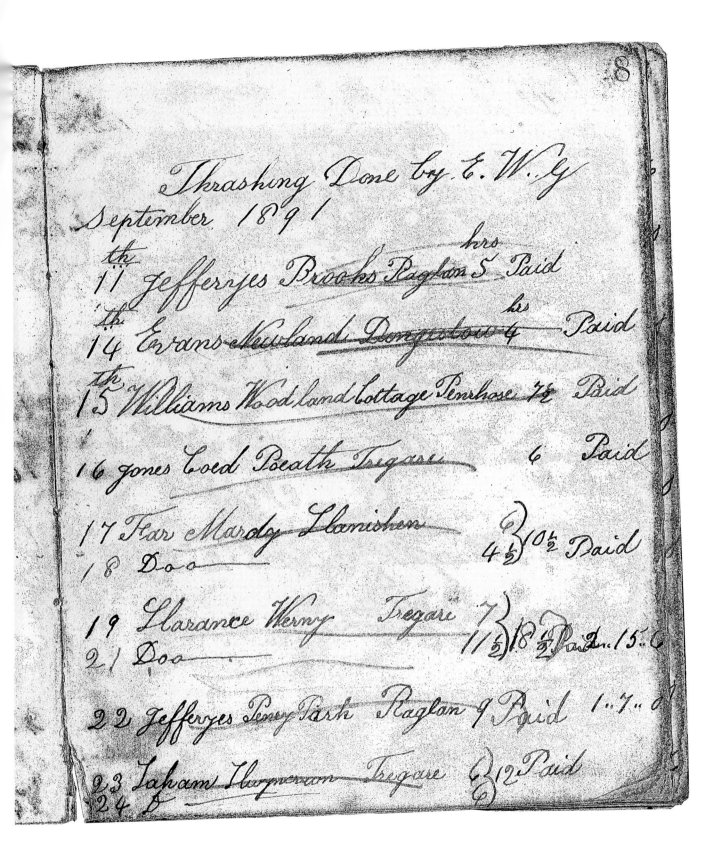

Thrashing Done by E. W. G

September 1891

11th Jefferyes Brooks Raglan 5 hrs Paid

14th Evans Newland Dingestow 4 hrs Paid

15th Williams Woodland Cottage Penrhose 7½ Paid

16 Jones Coed Boeath Tregare 6 Paid

17 Far Mardy Llanishen
18 Do 4½ 10½ Paid

19 Llarance Werny Tregare 7
21 Do 11½ 18½ Paid 2..15..6

22 Jefferyes Perry Park Raglan 9 Paid 1..7..0

23 Laham Hungerson Tregare 12 Paid
24 Do

This first page of Enoch William Griffiths account book showing details of thrashing undertaken by him commencing on September 11, 1891. On this, his first season he undertook a total of 1,050 hours thrashing at 3/- per hour, totalling £157.10s.0d.

No. 11   Steam Roller

Mr Pardoe

1st May 99	Repairing regulating valve				
	3 h @ 9d per hour	£		9	9
2nd May	Paid			9	0
	Emery for grinding down			1	6
	and asbestos joint twine				6
	Cheque by post 25th July 1899	£	1	0	9

23 June 99	Taking out front Rolls preparing				
	two men to scurf Boiler including				
	travelling time 12 hrs			9	0
24th	Making 1 Steam Joint & 1 Big Dome				
	Joint including travelling time 12 hrs			9	0
	1 Piece of asbestos				11
26th	Refixing front Rolls making up				
	joints & examining gearing 8 hrs			6	0
	2 5/8 nuts				2
		£	1	5	1
26	Two Bushes Supplied			6	0
			1	11	1

Paid
Cheque per post 14 Oct 1899

545

Account entry for repairs carried out to Monmouthshire County Council's Steam Roller No.2 in 1899.

Above: E. & O. Griffiths of Dingestow acquired their first petrol-engined motor lorry in the early 1930s, a Willys Overland Crossley three-way tipper supplied new. Left: Oliver's son Derek is seen infront of the Willys Overland Crossley tipper at Dingestow.

Overleaf: This Sentinel DG6 6wl steam tipper DG3171 is seen with a 1930 Willys Overland Crossley 'Manchester' 4 wheeler WO4204 in the background.

Entering service on April 22, 1931 this Foden 'Speed 6' steamer WO5273 was subsequently sold to William Hancock & Co. Ltd., The Brewery, Cardiff, and used thereafter as a drawbar outfit. It is seen above with Oliver's daughter and opposite with his son Derek.

In 1934 they acquired an 8 wheel Sentinel S8 steam lorry, UJ3652. This vehicle was a flatbed, and was an ex-demonstrator model purchased through Wm. Fish of Bristol. The vehicle is believed to be the only example of the Sentinel 8wl steamer to survive.

1935.
1934.

May.   Order no K/2.
            To hauling from Cwmnypscoy Quarry to
            Rock   d. - Hilston Rd.
1st. to 2nd.   98 ton 3q.   2½ stones.   22 mls.
                7   3q.
            105 " 16   "   "   22 mls @ 3/4.   17 12 8

            Order. no. K. 17.
            To hauling from Cwmnypscoy. Quarry
May.   Rockfield Hilston Rd.
26 to 30th   38 ton 2 cwt. 2½ Stone. 22 mls @ 3/4.   6   7 0

May.   Order. no. M.R. 320.
            From Cwmnypscoy to Bryndu...
            8 ton 19 cwt. ⅕ to Dust. 23 mls @ 3/6.   1 11 4
                                        a/c. Rend. 31.5.34.

            Order. no. K/17.
June. 1st to 5th Ex. Cwm Quarry to Hilston
                43 ton 1 cwt 1q. 2½.Stone.
    " " "   28 ton 2 cwt.   2½   "
    " 8th - 11th   16 ton 19 cwt. 2q. 2½ Stone.
    " 15th - 19th   43 ton 17 cwt 3q. 2½ Stone.
    " 23rd   13 ton 2 cwt 2q.
    " 28th   8 " 5 " 0
                153 " 8 " 0   2½ Stone at. 22 mls at. 3/4. £25 11 4.

            Order. K/30.
            Ex Cwmnypscoy Quarry. to Hilston.
27th to 30th   40 ton 18 cwt. 2q. ¾ stone. 22 mls. at. 3/4. £6 16 5.

70

1926.   Order no K/302.
                      To hauling from Cwmynyscoy Quarry
                      to Porthygaelod — Skenfrith Rd.
Jan 14th/22nd. 41 ton 19 cwt. 0 q.   B. Ballast.
     " 30th   10 ton 2 cwt. 0 q.   "   " .
     " 31st   17 ton 17 cwt. 1 q.   "   " .
                 69 ton 18 cwt. 1 q.   24 mls.   4/6. 15 14 6

                      Order. no. K/297.
                      To hauling from Cwmynyscoy Quarry
                      to Llanvetherine — Llandeilo Road.
Feby. 3rd/17th.   73 ton 10 cwt.   B. Ballast.   19 mls @   3/8 £13 9 6

                      Order. no. K/331.
                      To hauling from Cwmynyscoy Quarry
                      to Triley — Llanvihangel Rd.
Feby. 6th/7th. 23 ton 18 cwt. 1 q.   1½" to dust.   13 mls. at. 2/7. £3 1 9.

                      Order. no. K/302.
                      To hauling from Cwmynyscoy Quarry
                      to Porthgaelod — Skenfrith. Rd.
Feby
131st 8th   90 ton 12 cwt. 3 q.   B. Ballast.   24 mls
10th/11th   20 ton 14 cwt. 0 q.   "   "
8th/10th   15 ton 15 cwt. 0 q.   "   "
15/19th   107 "   6 "   1
                 234 "   8 "   0 q.   B. Ballast. 24 mls.   4/6. 52 14 9.

Opposite, above and *overleaf*: Examples of accounts showing work carried out for Monmouthshire County Council at Cwmynyscoy Quarry, Pontypool are given for the four year period from 1934.

1937.

Order. no. K. 522.
To hauling from Cwmynyscoy Quarry to
St. Maughns Rd.

April 5th   10 ton 19 cwt   2g. B.B.   26 mls.   4/7. £2

Order. no. K. 524.
To hauling from Cwmynyscoy Quarry to
Bryndewi.

April
15th 20th   100 ton 3 qwt'.   2¼ Stone.   26 mls.   3/1   15
16th 24th   30 ton 10 cwt'.   8 to dust'.   19 mls. 19.   3/1   4

Order. no. K. 527.
To hauling from Cwmynyscoy Quarry to
St. Maughns.

April.
20th. 26th.   49 ton 17 cwt. 3g.   2¼ Stone.   26 mls.   4/3. 10
13th. 19th.   50 ton 13 cwt 2g.   B.B.   26 mls.   4/7. £11
29th   8 ton 8 cwt.   Dust.   26 mls.   4/3. 1   1

Order. no. K. 534.
To hauling from Cwmynyscoy Quarry to
Llwynfrank Road.

2bt'. 24th.   12 ton 7 cwt'.   quarry cleanings.   14 mls 9/10   1   1.

Order. No. K. 533.
To hauling from Cwmynyscoy Quarry to
Llwynfrank Rd.

1987

Order. no. K. 530.
To hauling from Cwmynyscoy Quarry to
Llangattock - Lingoed.

2nd ft.   64 Ton 15 cwt. 3q.   B. Spalls.
30 ft.   29 · 11 · 3
          94 Ton 7 " 2   B. B.   19 mls.   3/5. £ 16 12 8.

Order. no. K. 530.
To hauling from Cwmynyscoy Quarry to
Llangattock - Lingoed.

7th.   53 Ton 17 cwt. 1q.   B. B.   19 mls.   at.   3/5. £ 9 4 0.

Order. no. K. 527.
To hauling from Cwmynyscoy Quarry to
St. Maughns.

5th 22nd.   22 Ton 13 cwt 2q.   8. dust.   26 mls.   4/3. £ 4 16 4.

Order. no. K. 554.
To hauling from Cwmynyscoy Quarry to
St. Maughns.

6th. 10th.   99 Ton 5 cwt. 1q.   B. B.   26 mls. at.   4/7. £ 22 14 5.

Order. no. K. 559.
To hauling from Cwmynyscoy Quarry to
Brynderi.

4th. 16th.   100 Ton 17 cwt.   B. B.   19 mls. 3/5.   £ 17 4 7.

Order. no. K. 56. 8.
To hauling from Cwmynyscoy Quarry to
St. Maughns.

May,

This Marshall Agricultural steam threshing machine was bought new on September 1, 1932 and was used up to and throughout the Second World War. It had an Unladen weight of 8 tons 11 cwt.

Overleaf: It is seen working on the drum at Blue Door Farm, Dingestow.

Willy Overland Crossley petrol-engined 4wl tipper on demonstration from the manufacturer.

Above: Wartime view of Bedford tipper BCJ184 with Les Chilcott.

Left: Oliver Griffiths at Efailnewydd, Dingestow just before nationalisation. Around 1950 Enoch and Oliver Griffiths bought Cwmynyscoy Quarry following the nationalisation of their haulage fleet. It was to be a profitable period of trading with the development of Cwmbran New Town.

Overleaf and Pages 82-83: Views of the Cwmynyscoy Quarry at Pontypool.

This 4wl Dodge tipper VAX439 was driven by Bert PUGH.

Tipper OAX524 was operated on council road repairs.

Twins Andrew and Richard Griffiths on the bonnet of Bedford "J" type.

Leyland tipper working out of Ifton Quarry and driven by Les Hitchings.

A Cat 992 loading shovel driven by Tom Griffiths clearing snow at the Keepers at Blaenavon.

An AEC Marshall 6wl Bulk tipper engaged on the carriage of foundry coke.

Two Dodge tippers being loaded with gravel from the bed of the River Wye at Monmouth.

Atkinson 8wl Tipper BAX544K Driven by Malcolm Price delivering tarmac on the A38 at Gloucester.

Seddon Atkinson 8wl tipper at Praills Garage, Monmouth.

On his retirement, Derek's sons Richard and Andrew operated a single Foden 6wl tipper BFD226W on Llanwern Slag.

Long-serving driver Malcolm Price is seen with this ERF 6wl tipper EAG313Y.

LLANTILIO TRANSPORT, CLARRY WHISTANCE, ABERGAVENNY

Clarry Whistance's father lived at Llanvetherine, on the road from Abergavenny to Ross-on-Wye, and whilst he was involved in farming, he also operated as a haulage contractor in the transport of livestock.

In his youth, Clarry assisted his father in the transport business, but in 1971, just after his marriage to Edna, entered into business on his own account with a Bedford TK fitted with a detachable 16ft stock box. Living at Llantilio Croesenny, near Abergavenny, he traded as 'Llantilio Transport'.

Both he and Edna drove the vehicle, and they quickly expanded, using larger vehicles, including Bedford KM, Leyland and AEC 4 wheelers. With the increasing size of loads, and greater distances being covered they started to operate articulated outfits, at first an AEC, thence Volvo F86, F88 and F12 models. Eventually standardising on Scania, at first with 112 and 113 models, they now operate a modern fleet of Scania 124 tractor units with maximum capacity three and four deck stock semi-trailers, together with a 4 wheel Scania rigid.

Whilst Clarry and Edna still drive, their children Tina and John are very much involved in the business.

During the Foot & Mouth outbreak they carried out much flat work, an involvement mainly on hauling timber products, which they still maintain. Edna and John have been involved in carrying car parts into Germany from the U.K. Whilst serving livestock markets, they travel nationwide, even transporting sheep to and from winter keep. This is the practise of dairy farmers keeping their herds indoors in the winter months and letting their fields for grazing sheep mostly from upland farms and thereafter being returned to the upland in March and April for lambing, at home pastures.

The carriage of livestock requires a high degree of expertise, and great care is undertaken in loading in order to ensure due welfare of the animals. Anyone watching long serving driver John Pritchard loading would be pleased to see this knowledge being put to good use, showing him taking account of specific breeds and types and the individual capacity of individual trailers. Livestock transport is not easy work, and it is the knowledge and expertise of those involved which ensures the welfare of the animals.

Clarry Whistance and John Pritchard seen with this Scania 82M – 4 wheeler which was converted into a livestock lorry.

This Scania 4wl stock lorry N209XOL seen on the Lorry Wash at Abergavenny Cattle Market is normally driven by Clarry and Edna's daughter Tina.

Scania 113M articulated tractor unit N864JWT coupled to a three-deck triaxle livestock semi-trailer.

Scania 112M tractor units E180EFO and E200EFO seen at Llandewi Rhydderch.

Scania 113M – N372AVU at Abergavenny Cattle Market.

Seen at Abergavenny this Scania is coupled to a three-deck livestock trailer.

Four Scania Tractor Units forming part of the Llantilio Transport fleet.

Much flat work is carried out.

Above: Three-deck livestock semi-trailer.
Below: Four-deck livestock Stepframe semi-trailer.

Scania 124L tractor unit W257NTG seen at the Abergavenny lorry wash.

Thankfully John Whistance wasn't badly injured as first thought in this collision involving Scania Y603KUX. Trapped in the vehicle, when freed, he was conveyed to Hospital in the Air Ambulance. The vehicle was subsequently rebuilt.

Two Scania 124L tractor units Y603KUX and T412JAW.

Another pair of Scania 124L tractor units S543FUB and T412JAW. Llantilio Transport have standardised on the Scania model for some years. Clarry and Edna Whistance and their children Tina and John are actively involved in the business.

CLIFFORD LLEWELLYN, LLANGATTOCK LINGOED

Clifford Llewellyn spent his youth working on farms, and eventually set himself up as a farm contractor, at first using horses but thereafter motor tractors. He bought the Hendre Farm, Llangattock Lingoed, and subsequently added Great Park Farm, Llanvihangel Crucorney, and a large section of Little Park Farm, and other parcels of accommodation land, totalling over 400 acres.

Against this background he bought a small Austin flatbed lorry, with a detachable livestock box, and started hauling to and from local cattle markets, and for local farmers.

Married, Cliff had five children – David, Gwyn, Richard, Susan and Caroline.

Having bought his first lorry, the Austin, from Jack Davies with its carrier's licence; he thereafter bought an ex-WD Bedford OWLD in Nottingham, applied for a 'B' licence allowing him to haul within a 25 mile radius on livestock and agricultural produce, and fitted it with a new stock box manufactured by Carmichael of Worcester.

He obtained a contract to carry livestock for FMC and expanded this part of his business. He bought a Thames Trader from Cyril Lane of W.G. Lane & Sons, Abergavenny, 545HAX in 1963 and transferred the stock box to it. Expansion saw him running four vehicles, and although others drove for him, sons David, Gwyn and Richard were involved in the business.

On May 4, 1994 Cliff died at 71 years of age, but his widow kept the business going for a while. Eventually they withdrew from haulage, and another Monmouthshire transport business had disappeared.

Clifford Llewellyn's main achievement had been to build up a farming enterprise based on over 400 acres, a big holding, even for these days.

Above left: Modern Bedford TK livestock lorry EYB309J with new box.

Above right: Another Bedford XRP359J with Cliff Llewellyn's grand-daughter.

Opposite above: This Leyland Livestock lorry OHY783R is seen at Great Park Farm, Llanvihangel Crucorney.
Right: Clifford Llewellyn's son David subsequently entered business as a general haulage contractor, but also dealing with animal feeds, hay & straw, fertiliser and shavings. This Seddon Atkinson VFK193X is fitted with a high tailboard to help facilitate the carriage of high loads of hay and straw.

With previous owners livery this Seddon Atkinson YWE29T was normally used for on-field collections of hay and straw.

Not carrying steel this Seddon Atkinson 4wl Flat E340VVM was loading on-field, big bales of straw.

Three Seddon Atkinson 4 wheelers owned by D. J. Llewellyn – E340VVM, B988VHW and B982VHW, seen at Great Park Farm, Llanvihangel Crucorney.

This ERF E6 4 wheeler H866HLR was fitted with a Cummins 210 Engine.

WILLIAM STEDMAN, TALYWAIN

The origins of the well known 'Stedman' business goes back four generations. Page Stedman was born at Bristol, but with the sad death of his mother he was taken to Talywain as an infant and brought up by his mother's childless sister and her husband.

He was brought up in a public house, The Greyhound Hotel, Pisgah Road, Talywain, and when old enough was responsible for fetching cider from Hereford, not only for their own pub but also for other licensed premises in the area. This was done with a horse and cart, and saw his entry into haulage for others in the area, carrying hay and straw, domestic coal to individual householders, and anything that needed to be transported.

Page's son William Wright Stedman followed his father into the business, and from the early 1930s a substantial fleet of lorries was being used, mostly based on a Morris Commercial chassis. Eventually furniture removals, meat haulage to local butchers, hay, straw and shale for use in brickmaking were being transported. A taxi business was set up and coaches were soon being operated. It was the full type of local transport business, and the cider was still being collected from Bulmers at Hereford much of which was for sale into the licensing trade.

William Wright Stedman had three sons, and whilst all three were expected to help in the business, it was William Spencer Stedman (born 1925) who eventually took over the haulage business. Brothers Page and Robert Charles became individually involved in grocery businesses, but Robert thereafter moved on to run a property business.

William was joined in the haulage business by his sons (4th generation) Philip and Christopher, but in the early 1970s they withdrew from transport and sold the vehicles and disposed of the coal round. They had taken premises at the former Star Brick & Tile Company's site, now known as the Star Trading Estate. Thereafter father and sons concentrated on the supply of wine, spirits, beer and drinks to the licensing trade, a business that had been carried on by four generations. Expansion saw William Stedman's as one of the largest independent suppliers to the trade within South Wales.

With William's sad death in January, 1988 at 62 his sons Philip and Christopher carried on the venture which continued to expand.

However, in 2003 the brothers sold the business and the trading name of William Stedman to the well-known Cardiff brewers S.A. Brain & Co. Ltd., and as such it continues to thrive.

Philip and Christopher, with offices at the Star Trading Estate, Ponthir, now trade as Stedman Brothers (Events) Ltd., and operate six converted airport buses as outside bars at tournaments and events throughout South Wales and the South West and Midlands.

Thus the respected 'Stedman' name continues in business, having descended in Monmouthshire (Gwent) through four generations.

MAN 4wl covered lorry F746AUH at the Star Trading Estate, Ponthir.

This Wm. Stedman Leyland Daf Curtainsider J29UWO seen at Ponthir.

Another Leyland Daf P835WBO owned by Wm. Stedman Ltd.

Stedman's Daf curtainsider in Cross Street, Abergavenny, outside the Town Hall.

Owned by Stedman Brothers Events this mobile bar is in travelling mode and is actually a converted bus.

"It's Brains you want". A mobile bar set out in the picturesque surroundings of 'The Rolls of Monmouth Golf Club'.

A mobile bar set out at an event at Cardiff Castle.

CLIFF STEPHENS TRANSPORT, GRIFFITHSTOWN, PONTYPOOL

The origins of the Stephens' business can be traced back to the 1920s. The earliest record I have actually been able to find is on December 31, 1931 when Joseph George Stephens of Redwood Villas, Commercial Street, Griffithstown bought a Morris truck WO5942 with an unladen weight of 1 ton 8 cwt from Gwyns' Garage at Ystrad Mynach. He operated in a small way initially, but with the arrival of his sons Granville and Clifford in the business expanded, carrying household removals, light haulage and domestic coal deliveries, now trading as J.G. Stephens & Sons.

With the death of their father, Granville and Cliff carried on the business, and in the early 1950s expanded into steel haulage out of the Panteg Works of Richard Thomas & Baldwin. Eventually the coal round and vehicles were disposed of and traded thereafter as Knights' of Sebastopol. Granville became responsible for the household removals side of the business, while brother Cliff handled the steel traffic.

Eventually the steel transport was transferred to a limited company – Cliff Stephens Transport Ltd. with both brothers as directors and sole shareholders, whilst the removals side remained as a partnership between them, but still trading as J.G. Stephens & Sons. The removal fleet consisted of four pantechnicons – all Bedfords, whilst the steel traffic was carried out with a fleet of four vehicles also. Two AEC Mammoth Major 8wl rigids and two four wheelers eventually giving way to articulated vehicles.

With the death of Cliff, the business carried on for a while, but in 1971 the removal business, vehicles, premises and depot at Griffithstown, and the trading name of J.G. Stephens & Sons, passed to Roy Fox who thereafter traded as 'Fox the Mover' with part of his fleet, and with the other part for a time as J.G. Stephens & Sons. Eventually, as he expanded, the trading name of Stephens was allowed to lapse, and the two businesses merged.

Bill (William) Gibbon had driven for the Stephens' brothers since 1952 on the steel traffic out of Panteg Steelworks, and in 1971 with Granville eager to retire, bought his house at Cambria Street, Griffithstown, and the steel transport business with its remaining two articulated vehicles – Both ERFs.

Bill's sons Clive and John both went to work for their father, John arriving in 1973. Eventually Bill decided to retire, and in 1987 John (William John Gibbon) bought the business off his father – thereafter still trading as Cliff Stephens Transport Ltd with wife Paula and himself as directors.

They built up the business, standardising on ERF until the fleet amounted to ten vehicles. Continuing to haul out of Panteg Steelworks – a stainless steel plant – originally Richard Thomas & Baldwin, thence British Steel Corporation and finally as Avesta. Much of the work was hauling to Avesta's Sheffield plant for finishing, and came back with whatever was on offer, which on occasions was plant to Ross-on-Wye. Whilst Clive continued driving for him, John's son Luke started in 2000.

In 2002 Christian Salveson took over the contract for transport out of Panteg, and in consequence John and his wife sold off most of the fleet – the drivers transferring to Salvesons. They kept two of the ERFs, and thereafter often loaded out of Panteg but through Salvesons. After a year the contract passed to Stillers Carline and he and son Luke continued driving the two ERF 'E' series tractor units mostly out of Panteg.

Alas, the announcement was made that production was ending at Panteg, and the last coil was produced on March 19, 2004. Fittingly this last coil was loaded on a trailer drawn by John's ERF. Sadly on that date the last two vehicles were taken off the road, sold, and Cliff Stephens Transport subsequently wound up. Thus, not only had a long-established and respected transport business gone, but with the closure of Panteg Steelworks yet another part of South Wales' Industrial Heritage had disappeared.

FLEET LIST

Index No.	Type	Notes
AWO548K	ERF 4x2 artic	Gardner 180
TDW598J	ERF 4x4 artic	Gardner 180. From Syd Jenkins, Newport
KTX730P	ERF 4x2 artic	Gardner 240. New from South Wales Commercials, Newport
OFM579P	ERF 4x2 artic	Cummins 250. ERF demonstrator from South Wales Commercials, Newport
XHB750T	ERF 4X2 artic	Cummins 250. New from South Wales Commercials, Newport
CBO776V	ERF 4x2 artic	Cummins 290. New from South Wales Commercials, Newport
JTG212W	ERF 4x2 artic	Cummins 240T. New from Richard Read (Commercials) Ltd., Longhope
BYA802X	ERF 4x2 artic	Cummins 240T. From Cowbridge area
A379UUH	ERF 4x2 artic	Cummins 290. New from South Wales Commercials, Newport
A86WBO	ERF 6x2 artic	Cummins 350. From Nestle, Chepstow
A89WBO	ERF 6x2 artic	Cummins 350. From Nestle, Chepstow
B494ANY	ERF 4x2 artic	Cummins 320. New from South Wales Commercials, Newport
C616GBO	ERF 4x2 artic	Cummins 320. New from South Wales Commercials, Newport
D706AFL	ERF 6x2 artic	Cummins 320. From Knowles Wisbiech
E178BRS	ERF 6x2 artic	Cummins 320.
E977UDS	ERF 6x2 artic	Cummins 350. From Langdon, Avonmouth
F37CNY	ERF 4x2 artic	Cummins 320. New from South Wales Commercials, Newport
F137PAY	ERF 6x2 artic	Cummins LT325
G69MSA	ERF 6x2 artic	Cummins 380. From Wye Commercials, Ross-on-Wye; ex-Forfar Haulage
J268CGU	ERF 6x2 artic	Perkins 340. From Wye Commercials, Ross-on-Wye
K136HSA	ERF 6x2 artic	Cummins 320. From Wye Commercials, Ross-on-Wye; ex-Aberdeen Haulage
K410DEH	ERF 6x2 artic	Perkins 330. Demonstrator from Richard Read (Commercials) Ltd., Longhope
M209VTU	ERF 6x2 artic	Cummins 380. From Wye Commercials, Ross-on-Wye
M855FKH	ERF 6x2 artic	Cummins 380. From Wye Commercials, Ross-on-Wye; ex-Goole area
M254RSX	ERF 6x2 artic	Cummins 410. From Wye Commercials, Ross-on-Wye; ex Scottish vehicle
N828BSC	ERF 6x2 artic	Cummins 380. From Wye Commercials, Ross-on-Wye; ex Scottish vehicle
P273EVO	ERF 6x2 artic	Cummins 380. From Wye Commercials, Ross-on-Wye; ex Meacher, Southampton – although one of six operated from Derby
P137KYA	ERF 4x2 artic	Perkins 340. From Wye Commercials, Ross-on-Wye; ex-Wincanton Transport

Six ERF tractor units in the Cliff Stephens Transport fleet E977UDS, F37CNY, E178BRS, C616GBO, A86WBO and A89WBO.

ERF 'C' Series 4x2 Articulated tractor unit BYA802X

This ERF E14 tractor unit E977UDS was a 6x2 model.

The Cliff Stephens fleet was standardised on ERF for 35 years. This line of vehicles is seen with John Gibbon at Panteg Steelworks.

This ERF outfit approaches Panteg Steelworks from the South in June, 1994.

This ERF EC14, N828BSC is seen delivering plant at Ross-on-wye.

Stephen's ERF, G69MSA travelling Westbound on the M4 Motorway at Magor in April, 1998.

Another view of the ERF N828BSC with plant at Ross-on-Wye.

The last coil of steel to leave Panteg Steelworks at 12.30 pm on March 19, 2004. Seen from the left: Kevin Johnson, in charge of Logistics, loader Alwyn Marwood, John Gibbon and loader Pat Longthorn.

The last coil to leave Panteg is carried on a trailer drawn by John Gibbon's tractor unit.

Whilst the last coil was loaded out of Panteg Steelworks on March 19, 2004, it coincided with the closure of the Cliff Stephens business, John and Luke Gibbon are shown in the lower photograph.

Panteg Steelworks

P.M. HEATON PUBLISHING

Paul Heaton was born at New Inn, Pontypool, in 1944 and was educated at Greenlawn Junior School in New Inn and the Wern Secondary School at Sebastopol. At fifteen he commenced employment, at first in a local store and then with a builder's merchant. A year later he was appointed as a Deck Cadet in the Merchant Navy, with the Lamport & Holt Line of Liverpool, and served in their vessels *Chatham, Constable* and *Romney* usually in the Brazil and River Plate trades. He joined the Monmouthshire Constabulary (now Gwent) in 1963, and served at Abergavenny, Cwmbran, Newport, the Traffic Department, the Motor Cycle Section, as the Press Liaison Officer, and for five years represented Inspectors for the whole of Wales nationally on the Joint Central Committee of the Police Federation. He was promoted to sergeant in 1974 and Inspector in 1982. On his retirement he served as Market Inspector with the RSPCA for eight years and at the same time was Landlord of a Public House for three years. He has always maintained an interest in maritime history and in transport generally, and has had the following books published:

Reardon Smith 1905-1980 (1980)
The Baron Glanely of St. Fagans and W.J. Tatem Ltd., with H.S. Appleyard (1980)
The 'Redbrook', A Deep-Sea Tramp (1981) four editions
The 'Usk' Ships (1982) two editions
The Abbey Line (1983)
Kaye, Son & Co. Ltd., with K. O'Donoghue (1983)
Reardon Smith Line 1984) two editions
The South American Saint Line (1985)
Welsh Blockade Runners in the Spanish Civil War (1985)
Lamport & Holt (1986) two editions
Tatems of Cardiff (1987)
Booth Line (1987)
Jack Billmeir, Merchant Shipowner (1989)
Welsh Shipping, Forgotten Fleets (1989)
The Gallant Ship 'Stephen Hopkins' with R.J. Witt (1990)
Palm Line, with Laurence Dunn (1994)
Not All Coppers Are...! (1994)
Wynns – The First 100 Years for John Wynn (1995) three editions
Wynns – The Last 20 Years for John Wynn (1996)
L.C. Lewis, Heavy Haulage (1996)
Wynns Overseas first draft for John Wynn (1998)
The Wynns Fleet – 120 Years of Road Haulage (2003)
Lamport & Holt Line (2004)
Road Transport Gwent (2004)
Road Transport – The Read Story (2005)
Road Transport Monmouthshire (2005)
Road Transport Wales & Border (2005)